# A Scent of Rain

*Sowing the seeds of revival across Uganda*

Dalen Garris

## A Scent of Rain

Copyright @ 2017 by Dalen Garris

All rights reserved. No portion of this book may be reproduced, stored in a retrieval system, or transmitted in any form or by any means—electronic, mechanical, photocopy, recording, scanning, or other—except for brief quotations in critical reviews or articles, without the prior written permission of the publisher.

Unless otherwise noted Scripture quotations are taken from the King James Version.

Scripture quotations marked ESV are taken from THE ENGLISH STANDARD VERSION @ 2001 by Crossway Bibles, a division of Good News Publishers.

Printed in the United States of America

All rights reserved.

ISBN-13:9780999469415
ISBN-10:099946941X

# DEDICATION

To the children.

It is the children who will experience the rain and will take this great harvest to the rest of the world.

# Table of Contents

|    | Preface                      | Pg vi |
|----|------------------------------|-------|
| 1  | Greetings from Eastern Uganda | Pg 1  |
| 2  | Kaberamaido                  | Pg 3  |
| 3  | Kaberamaido, Day 2           | Pg 6  |
| 4  | Soroti and Kaberamaido       | Pg 9  |
| 5  | Day 4 and 5 in Soroti        | Pg 12 |
| 6  | The Scent of Rain            | Pg 16 |
| 7  | Kumi, Day 1                  | Pg 18 |
| 8  | Kumi, Day 2                  | Pg 20 |
| 9  | Resistance in Kumi           | Pg 23 |
| 10 | A Flat Day in Kumi           | Pg 25 |
| 11 | Funeral in Kumi              | Pg 28 |
| 12 | A Note from Cindy            | Pg 30 |
| 13 | Into Southern Uganda         | Pg 32 |
| 14 | Cindy Again                  | Pg 34 |

| 15 | On to Western Uganda | Pg. 36 |
| 16 | In Kihihi | Pg. 38 |
| 17 | Holding Back the Rain | Pg. 42 |
| 18 | The Hem of His Garment | Pg. 44 |
| 19 | Back in Mbarara | Pg. 48 |
| 20 | Delivering the Message | Pg. 51 |
| 21 | Intensity in Mbarara | Pg. 53 |
| 22 | Cindy and Diana | Pg. 55 |
| 23 | Royalty in God | Pg. 58 |
| 24 | Healings and One-liners | Pg. 62 |
| 25 | Miracles and Anointing | Pg. 64 |
| 26 | Going Home | Pg. 67 |
|  | About the Author | Pg. 69 |

# Preface

The year before I took this journey to Uganda, I answered an email by a young pastor who wanted to bring revival to his country but didn't know how to do it. A one line email – that's all he sent me, but it was the feeling that underlined it and an unmistakable nudge from the Holy Spirit that told me to answer this call. I am so glad I did.

While waiting for him at the airport, I ran into Bishop Girado as we both were trying to purchase airtime at one of the kiosks there. We hit if off immediately and set up the campaign right then and there that is described in the first part of this book. Pastor Noah showed up minutes later, and we set up the campaign for the latter half of this story.

I have been to Uganda many time since, but this trip more than any other has always felt like the foundational trip that set the stage for all the others that would come later. It was on this trip that our focus was set and our vision was planted. I could feel the weight of something great, the enormity being hidden but felt nonetheless. Something was about to be created that was bigger than a simple evangelistic trip to an African nation in darkness. The harvest of revival was coming. I could hear the sound of an abundance of rain. It wasn't here yet but it was coming. The famine and drought were about to end.

There was a scent of rain.

# 1
# Greetings from Eastern Uganda

We just finished up three days of double services, a radio broadcast and main church service on Sunday. I still haven't adjusted to the jet lag so I'm pretty whooped … that is until it is time to go to sleep, which is when all of a sudden I wake up. <grimace>

We have gotten off to a slow start, but while that always worries me, it is pretty much par for the course. The second day, however, much more passion rose for both services. It was really good – not great, mind you, but better than anything we've seen in America for a long while.

But the third day, we went through the roof! In the morning service, I could feel the Spirit pouring out of me. Wow. I was pretty excited. The people were pretty excited also. But for the afternoon, which was the last service for the three days, I didn't even preach! I prayed over the bishops and anointed them with oil, then I made them pray over the pastors and anoint them. Then I was going to have the pastors turn around and pray over and anoint the people like I had done in Burundi, but I felt a strong leading not to do that. The people needed the inspiration to come from me praying over them, so for an hour or so, we prayed and prayed and prayed. You would have loved being there, getting your hands full of oil, pouring out your heart in prayer over each and every one of them, and feeling that miraculous flow of the anointing through your hands. Wow, it was really, really cool!

A couple of days of rest and searching for a place to buy Bibles and then it is off to the next city for four days. Usually, the momentum builds during this time, and you'd think that was a little strange seeing that God doesn't need to build momentum, but that seems to be the way it goes. I guess I'm the one that needs the runway to take off on. <grin>

The Catholic and the Anglican churches have a strong hold on this society and they are strongly prejudiced against the Pentecostal born-again churches. Under Idi Amin, they rejoiced when they saw Pentecostal churches burning, and they are only marginally better these days. The President of the country is born-again and is greatly loved here, so that should bring some change, but there are deeply rooted strongholds that have a firm grip on this society.

But we have the power! And the Glory! And the Anointing of the Holy Ghost! Watch for the miracles to follow. They are already being manifested in the south where the pastors that I visited last year are burning for revival and taking it to the streets. God is beginning to move in Uganda.

Did I mention that I am excited?

# 2
# Kaberamaido

I was greeted today like I have never been greeted before. These people were so excited to see me that it was somewhat humbling.

We are 50 km from the nearest city and 30 km from the nearest paved road, but there are people living all over here in the bush. During the hour long ride over dirt roads through the scrubby bush country, I was told that there are no more dangerous animals here – only pythons, which live under anthills and spring on unsuspecting people who walk by. Oh, that's nice to know. I don't think I'll be taking a walk through the bush anytime soon.

As we arrive, however, there are dozens of young girls coming out to greet me dressed in bright blue dresses with garlands made from bright pink flowers, yelling and waving their hands. Loud in the background is that strange high-pitched warbling that the women

here in Africa do. It's deafening. It is as if they were welcoming royalty or some homecoming national hero. I feel a bit unsettled but my host, Bishop Girado, tells me that I have to get out of the car so they can welcome me into the church.

This is not what I expected or what I am prepared for, but I sheepishly enter the tent they have set up. I have come to preach revival, plain and simple. I am not here to build churches or conduct city-wide crusades – I am here to ignite those who will. I am preaching a strong message that will wake up and ignite the churches here and inspire those "John the Baptists" that I know are here to rise up and set their country on fire with the outpouring of the Holy Spirit. An entrance such as what I experienced today was not part of that.

Nevertheless, I know that it is a demonstration of how much these people are hungry for God, even way out here where you would not expect to find many people. So I spent the afternoon with about 60 people, giving an overview of the vision I have, what I am going to show them out of the Word, and carefully leading them to

something new – a fierce driving to God to win souls and send revival.

I hope it works. This is not what I was ready for, and I'm not sure what I'm supposed to say anymore. Few people have Bibles, so I don't know how sophisticated their knowledge of the Scriptures is. Regardless, here I am, back in that ol' familiar situation where I have no idea what I am doing. Thanks a lot, God.

Sometimes I wonder if He thinks this is funny. I have no idea what to say, what message God wants for these people, or what I will be doing for the next 4 days. I only know I am here, that I really believe in the coming revival that I preach, and that I am expecting a supernatural outpouring of the Holy Ghost even way out here in the Bush. (Sigh) So here we go, stepping off into the unknown again.

We'll see what happens in the next four days. Will it be just an exciting time as they come to see the Muzumgu (white man) and leave entertained but not changed, or will God do something supernatural here that has not been seen in generations? If all I am here to do is entertain, then my mission has failed. "God, break the heavens and pour out the supernatural power of the Holy Spirit so that this world can see the reality of your Truth!" That's what I am here for.

# 3
# Kaberamaido, Day Two

It was a great day today in spite of the fact that my system is still upside down. I'm exhausted at 6 pm and wake up at 2:30 am. But that makes for some good reading and prayer time in the morning. And this morning's prayer hour was great. I know I'm ready to launch into today's messages ... I just don't know what they are yet.

The drive to the church we are holding services at is 1-1/2 hours long, and most of that is on dirt roads. We drive through an area that had been controlled by the Lord's Resistance Army (LRA) just a few years ago. The situation then was dire. Road blocks were set up everywhere, and if you were a young man or woman, you were taken for the army. If you were an white guy like me, well, let's just say you won't be coming home anytime soon. But those days are over to everyone's relief.

Once again, we are met on the road in front of the church by the children all dressed in blue waving flags in the air and singing and cheering. It makes you feel like a war hero coming home or something. You can tell they are genuinely excited as they accompany the car all the way up to the church. I got it on video this time. You are not going to believe it when you see it.

I am so completely out of my element here that I am totally reliant upon God to deliver the message. That's not just come cute "spiritual" saying – I really do not have a clue and it is a bit unsettling! This is not a meeting of pastors and church leaders, but of common people from all over the area. We are not in an urban area where the church can immediately affect the community around it, but in the middle of the bush where you can only guess that people

live around here. This is not the first time that God has placed me in this type of setting, but it just seems that the message I have to bring is not designed for this. I have no idea what these people need to hear ... but God does, and He drops the message on me as I stand up. Wow. Almost two hours later, the Spirit of the Lord has grabbed hold of hearts in a deep grip that even I don't understand.

The afternoon service is a repeat of the morning's. The message poured out of me like a river that kept flowing and would not stop. I can tell that these people are genuinely transformed. Something has happened here that is beyond my understanding. It's like God has a special thing going with these people but He hasn't let me in on it. I'm just the guy delivering the message. Gee, thanks.

I am really puzzled at this. It's obvious that it is no mistake that we are here in this outpost way out in the bush. Could it be that this is exactly how God does things? He confounds the wise and mighty and uses those humble vessels that depend upon Him to do great and mighty things. I honestly believe that God will raise up from this group of 100 or so people some mighty men and women who will make a significant impact on this country, and who knows? Maybe even the world. That would be just like Him, wouldn't it?

I have two more days of double services and the Sunday service to go yet. It ain't over yet.

# 4
# Soroti and Kaberamaido

Whew! What a day. I should've known right from the beginning that it was going to be a humdinger. The devil got up early and stayed up late, but he is such a punk that all he can do is trouble us but not stop us.

We had trouble the first thing in the morning. The Bishop locked the keys in the car! But you've got to hear this because this is

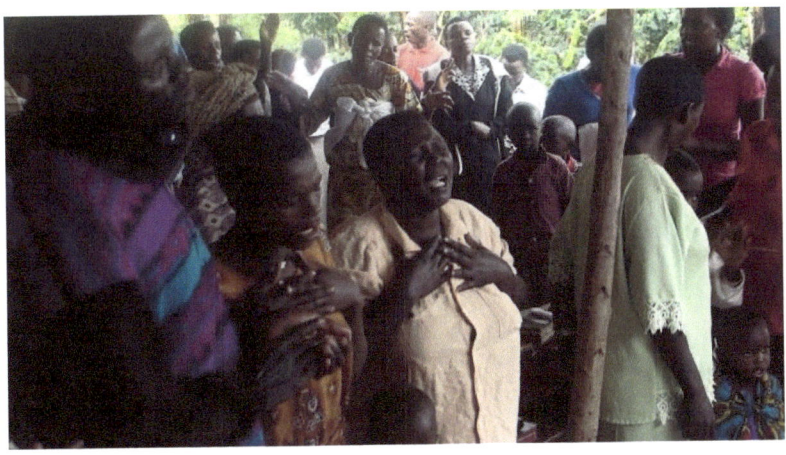

really funny: he was in the car and decided to check the water before he came to get me. Now, the keys are on one of those key fobs that have the buttons to lock and unlock the car, but this one is really squirrelly. The alarm is really unstable and often will go off all by itself. So the bishop gets out of the car, and – beep, beep – the car locks itself! Yeah, tell me that ain't the devil!

Okay, so we bind together in prayer, and the Lord brings him to someone who unlocks it. Good. We are off to the meeting. Now remember, we still have to drive an hour, and these people have been waiting all morning having slept there overnight on the floor of the church. But we get there and we get the same rambunctious greeting on the dirt path that we got yesterday. You gotta love these people!

The message poured out of me again. I had no idea where I was going next, but I just kept going! I love it when God does that. It's a little scary when you have no idea what you are going to preach

about, and you have to just swallow real hard, stand up, open your mouth, and hope something that makes sense comes out. But once I got on the horse, it was like riding a wild stallion. I could feel the fallow ground being broken in their hearts. This is what I've been struggling up against for two days, but finally it broke. As I called them forth to the altar, you could have heard their cries a mile away.

Broken, crucified prayer breaks up the fallow ground so that the seeds of the Word of God can be planted in their hearts, but it is the tears of repentance that waters the seeds that cause the harvest to spring forth out of the ground. Yeah, it was that good. It can only get better from here.

I should have known it wasn't over. Right after that, a pastor came up and told us the car had a flat. Now remember, we are 50 km from the nearest gas station, so there is no place and no electricity to get it repaired. The tire was just fine until we started breaking through to the Throne of God. <chuckle> Satan must have been livid!

But we manage to air up a spare (which was also flat) with a bicycle pump and we limped back to Soroti. I was so exhausted that I barely made it up the stairs to collapse on the bed. That's when you know you've put in a good day in the Lord.

This is the last day for this group. Nothing has gone the way I expected, none of the messages have been what I usually bring, so I would imagine that the results will be anything but usual or expected.

And that is something to smile about!

# 5
# Day 4 and 5 in Soroti, Uganda

Okay, I'm telling you ahead of time, that's it's going to be hard to believe all this stuff – I hardly believe it myself and I was there.

I have been in northern Uganda for the past two weeks -- a week in Tororo, and a week in the bush 50 km outside of Sororti. Last week was good, but it wasn't supernatural. If all I am coming here to do is to be good, then I have missed my mission. Ah, but this week, way out in the bush has been getting more and more powerful in an increasing crescendo since I got here.

Yesterday, the services weren't just pretty good, they were ... um ... supernatural! You know it's good when you feel like you are in the midst of a river in a raging torrent and are being carried downstream. About 10 souls got saved yesterday, which is great in itself. But more than that, a lot of these simple, country folk have been transformed. They may live way out in the bush, but they have a clear grip on the realities of life, and they fully understand what revival is, how much they need it, and what the price is that they will have to pay to receive it from God. Not many Christians in the USA are as sophisticated in this as they are.

Knowing the price and the desperation that is required to bring a true revival, they came up to the altar to commit their lives to whatever God asks them to do, no matter what the cost, no matter what it takes. You could feel the snap in the air as hearts broke before God. I anointed each one with oil and prayed down God's commission on each of them. These were serious people in a serious commitment. It was wonderful.

And then it started. I don't know how the healing line started, but once it got going, you couldn't stop it. Now, remember, I don't do tricks, miracles, or supernatural things. God told me once in Nigeria, "No miracles! If you do the miracles, they won't hear the message." (Yeah, I really did hear Him say that to me.) So I make no claims of the gift of healing to anybody. But this is not the first time that God has intervened anyway.

When I pray for healing, I like to ask them if they got healed. If they didn't, we pray some more. If they did, we move to the next one. At first it was headaches, and I've never met a headache that couldn't be healed. Then it moved on to bigger things. I knew we were on a roll when one lady told me as she came up that she didn't

need me to pray over her because she had already gotten healed just standing in the line! That's when I realized – OMG! -- every single person that came forward was getting healed!

And then the blind lady came up. Wow. She was over 80 years old. Her eyes had that milky white glaze over them and she could hardly see. By now, though, I am on a roll, so here goes … I anointed her eyes and prayed. When done, she starts to walk away and I stopped her. "Can you see?" "Yes, it's better."

I don't know where I got my holy boldness from, but I said, "Well, come back here. God doesn't do things half way." I kept thinking that even Jesus had to pray twice over that one guy. So we prayed again. And this time, she could see clearly. "Are you sure?" She looked at me with a grin that said of course she was sure! (Boy, did I feel stupid.)

Okay, I'm jazzed, right? But, oh man, today it gets even better because today they came and stood up to give testimonies of what happened yesterday. Someone who was deaf got healed, no less than three people who were crippled got healed, the blind lady can see, others had debilitating sicknesses that were washed away, and many others that I either could not understand or had an even harder time

believing. But I got most of them on video so that everyone will know that I'm not making this up! We are talking about over 50 miraculous healings! Everybody who came up got healed.

That ain't all. They have had a drought since September – not a drop of rain. Now, rain is a picture of revival. (Think Elijah on Mt. Carmel). Well, Bishop Girado Ukulol keeps saying that the rain has been following me like it did last week in Tororo. Today he pointed outside to the clouds that were forming. He said that the Bible says that the clouds are the dust of His feet, and that God was walking this way. Sure enough, right in the middle of my message, it started to rain. Not a whole lot, but it did rain. Now, that doesn't seem like a big deal to most of us, but to them, this was incredible because they haven't seen a drop for months! But get this! They had fully expected it! They knew it was going to rain while I was there because they were committed to revival. That's where the level of their faith is!

Right now it is 8 pm. I am back in my hotel in Soroti. Bishop Girado has gone back to his hometown to get his van to take me to the next place. They have just called to tell us that the people are still there in the church. Services ended 7 hours ago, but they say that the anointing of the Holy Spirit is still there and is so strong that no one wants to leave! Does that sound like something we've heard about in times past?

Brothers and sisters, keep praying and keep looking up. Revival is coming. It will come to Africa first, but God will use them to provoke the rest of the world to jealousy. The process here in Africa has begun. God is moving, and I have a feeling that no one has ever seen the power unleashed like it is about to be unleashed here in the (former) Dark Continent.

Please keep me in your prayers. My back is killing me, my guts are strained and hurting from standing so long, and I end each day in total exhaustion. But I gotta keep going. Please hold me up.

# 6
# The Scent of Rain

It rained today. I mean it rained! It was what we call in Texas, a Gully Washer! The thing is, here in northern Uganda where I am, it hasn't rained for months and everything is dry and dusty. This month was supposed to be the rainy season, but not only has there not been even a drop of rain or a hint of clouds, the forecast is for continued drought until at least the month of May sometime.

The problem is that their lives depend upon that rain. No rain; no crops. No crops; people starve.

I've been here for a week preaching revival. My message has

been simple and clear – revival is coming as it is written in the Books of Joel and Isaiah, but there is a price we as Christians must pay to receive it. But once it comes, it will be like a double portion of the latter rain. God is going to pour out the Latter Rain like we have never seen since the beginning of time!

Now, it's one thing to hear something like that, even when you can read it for yourself in the Word of God, but the reality of faith can sometimes struggle with wobbly legs to stand up on its own.

But then it rained today.

Yeah, you get the picture. When they saw the clouds gather, they got excited. When it started raining, they started believing. When a deluge started pouring down with wind and hail, they were hollerin', "It's a sign from God!"

Well, I'm not into stuff like that. I figure if it is a sign from God, great, but I have always figured that if He wanted me to know something, I reckon He'd tell me. If it's just some coincidence, well, that's okay. I'll take whatever help I can get.

The truth is, I ain't so sure it's <u>not</u> a sign from God. It might be just like Him to do something like this to get their attention. The people in this area of the world have seen much more than their share of trouble, and I guess that has a way of numbing you somewhat. They believe Brother Dale when he shows them in the Bible that revival is coming, and it's nice to hear that God is going to pour out His Spirit, but where was God when we were suffering and dying? It makes it a little tough to open up in simple naïve faith when the hearts of your people have been crushed.

Ah, but rain. Now that's something they can believe in. And not just rain, but a real Texas-sized Gully Washer!

Sometimes, you just gotta go with what God gives you.

# 7
# Kumi, Day 1

We had some great services today. We are about 8 km outside Kumi. It's a fairly big place, but only has walls and a partial roof – no windows, no floor, no doors, nothing but a huge shell of a building. About 100 people have filtered in by the end of the day, and they're expecting 300 people in the next day or so. African time is slow - there is no "hurry" in Africa. They'll get here when they get here.

The messages have been maturing over the years since I've started these Revival Campaigns. I am pulling stuff from new places in the Scriptures all the time and preaching it from brand new perspectives. All of this happens "on the fly", which means I'm getting the message at the same time that they are!

I'm running through money like water. Because of the extreme poverty out here, I need to provide food and other necessities for these people. They come here with nothing and sleep on the ground in the church overnight. The van we're using is old and beat up so we have to keep fixing one thing after another. (I should've just rented a car.) And Bibles are not cheap - IF you can find them. The language here is Ateso and the Uganda Bible Society won't have any in that language for another 2 months, so if they can be found, it is only at the bookstores, and they ain't cheap. And then there is always some unexpected expense that comes up.

I go from elation during services to bone tired and want-to-go-home at night. It's part of the adventure, I guess. But all you have to do is see the look on their faces the next day, and you are ready for more.

I would like to have a REAL cup of coffee, though… and a Big Mac. That would sure help a lot.

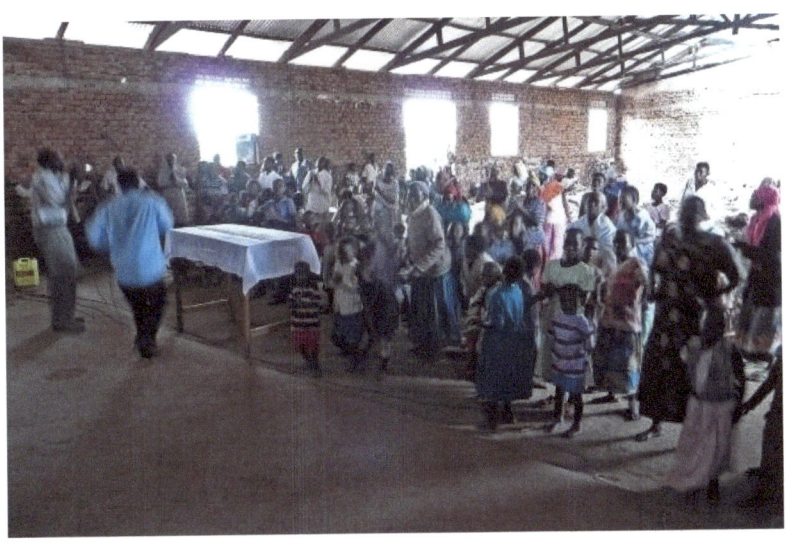

# 8
# Kumi, Day 2

It is the second morning here in Kumi, a small town here in northern Uganda. The landscape is identical to what I've seen throughout the country – dry red dirt with small brush interspersed with big Mango trees. Scattered throughout are little round huts made from mud bricks and straw roofs. It reminds me of the pictures I saw as a kid of the houses that the Three Little Pigs lived in.

The bishop I am with had a crusade here years ago and hundreds got saved. He says the Lord spoke to him to build a church here in the bush, not in the city. It is pretty big by Ugandan standards but it is only walls and a roof. The floor is made of hardened cow dung mixed with mud, which makes for a rock hard surface. There are no windows or doors, only openings in the walls. While it may seem crude, it works just fine. Africans don't need anything fancy to worship God – a lesson we could learn from them.

My challenge, however, is to break open their minds to grasp the enormity of what God is offering them. They are just like most of us whose eyes and ears are so used to "church as usual" that we have a hard time grasping the spiritual realities of Eternity. Our ears are stopped and our eyes are dim because the fallow ground of our hearts has not been broken up through repentance. We don't even know what to repent of, never mind that we even need to.

Yesterday, the Lord pierced their hearts with passage after passage that emphasized that if we do not win souls, we may not make it to Heaven. The whole idea of bringing forth fruit started with Rachael's cry in Genesis 30:1 and went through the parables, including the Good Samaritan which very clearly states that the answer to the lawyer's question of how do you gain Eternal Life is to win souls. Don't pass by the wounded sinners like the Priest (clergy) or the Levite (church person) do. From there we went through the True Vine, the Strait Way, The Church of Ephesus ... on and on, the Scriptures came forward and pierced them to the quick of their souls. Very simple – you say you want revival? Pay the price! You say you want to go to Heaven? Win souls. If you don't, your salt has lost its savour and you are good for nothing.

They get it. In America, I'd probably be thrown out the door for accusing and offending everyone there, especially the pastors. Here they cheer and fall to their knees in repentance. That's why revival will come here first, and then, if at all, maybe to America ... if America repents.

But first, I have to preach under the anointing so that God can open blind eyes, open the ears, and pierce their hearts. We're talking about bringing forth the Word that breaketh the rock in pieces. Dear God, please, please, please, give me the power to preach your Word like you would preach it!

Today will be Day 2 here in Kumi. I have no idea what God will bring forth; I only know that He cares a lot more for these people than I ever could, so I guess it's a safe bet to trust that He is going do something great.

# 9
# Resistance in Kumi

Never let it be said that serving the Lord is not a great adventure. It is also a battle. And that, I guess, is part of the adventure!

Just about every day, the devil hits us with something new. Usually it's the vehicle (which is what it is today), but Satan's imagination is not limited to that. It's always something new. He can't stop us, but he can sure vex and frustrate us. But the trick, I have learned, is to turn his attacks around on himself. So while I am stuck here at the hotel for 5 hours instead of being at the church preaching, I have decided to use this time that the devil has given me to storm the gates of Heaven for revival – right here, and right now! Revivals do not come without travailing intercessory groaning and desperate battles of prayer. I may not be an intercessor, but I do know that preaching without prayer is like the Meat Offering in Numbers 28. Without that pure, beaten oil to anoint it, it is dry, tasteless, and ineffective.

Perhaps, I should thank Satan for this time to cry out to God ... ummm ... perhaps not. <LOL>

Yesterday, the anointing filled the church so heavily that the bishop could actually see the glow of the Anointing. He was so excited (I mean like jumping-up-and-down excited) that I called home and had him tell Cindy about it. I didn't see it cause I was busy giving the message, but I could sure feel it. It was the presence of the Shekinah Glory. He could actually see the glow. Souls got saved, pastors came up with broken hearts to be anointed and prayed for, and the congregation felt the Holy Ghost conviction to repent. We broke through and something great happened.

The verse that kept resonating throughout the whole service was "the Lord is strong who executeth His Word". Amen. Don't make the mistake of not believing God. He is strong! And He WILL execute His Word because it is HIS Word. Praise God, revival is coming, yea, it is even here already!

And this was just the 2nd day in Kumi.

I am heading there now for the 3rd session. The van is finally fixed – this time it was the radiator, yesterday the brakes, flat tires, engine, gas, etc. But we are on our way. Just like that ol' Gospel song, "Praise God, I'm on my way to Canaan Land".

Do I sound excited? You have no idea. You'd have to be here to understand. As they say in Texas, "it's better felt than "telt".

# 10
# A Flat Day in Kumi

Day 3 in Kumi was incredible, but Day 4 was flat. Oh, I guess the message was good and all that, but the fire and power just seemed to be missing. Maybe it was just me. I'm sure if you asked the people, they would tell you how great services was, but it sure wasn't like yesterday ... at least to me anyway.

I struggled all the way to the hotel and into the night. Did I do something wrong? Maybe I got a little too cocky from yesterday's services and just expected the power to be right there at my fingertips. After so many years of this stuff, you'd think by now that I would have it down pat, but there is never a service that I go into that I am not nervous. I am constantly aware of how inadequate I am. Oh God, please send down the power! And He always does ... just some days more than others. But there is always a message. Always. And it is always the right one.

I think maybe I get so tense because so much is riding on it. I remember being told that mistakes in this business, unlike any other business, are fatal. Amen. We will make mistakes, but I don't want to minimize them by just assuming that God will cover them in the Blood just because.

Anyway, I was awake at 4 am and started praying. I'm not even sure I did anything wrong, but Lord, if I did, please forgive me for their sakes. And as I was praying, I started to laugh. It was like He was right there in the room. Everything was okay. It was cool. Just get up and keep doing what you're doing and remember ... it's not about you. (Yeah. Hold that thought.)

I've been reading some books from Leonard Ravenhill, and he really drives hard about prevailing prayer and intercessory prayer. It sure would be nice if I had some intercessory prayer warriors behind me – you know, the kind who travail in prayer through the night in agonizing battle to tear down strongholds. Yeah, we need some more of them. As I was reading I realized that I don't even know anyone who is an intercessory prayer warrior, not even one! Maybe they're there in secret like Elijah's 7,000. I sure hope so, because I could really use them to hold me up out here.

Anyway, today was much better. Yesterday the pastors wanted to be anointed with oil and prayed over. Today the people in the congregation came up. This is serious, covenant-making, dedication-type prayer. They know they are taking a step that they cannot ever go back on, but they are serious about this and want it sealed with the anointing.

And then, here comes the healing line ... Some folks have come here from the last place I was at, the church out in the bush, and told them about the healings we had there. These folks want the same thing to happen here. It doesn't seem that I have much of a choice in the matter, so we launched into it.

I used be able to feel the anointing as it flowed into the people I prayed for, sometimes like oil and sometimes like electricity, but lately I don't get to feel it as much. Once in a while is all. Today was like that. I prayed, I anointed, and they told me they were healed ... but I didn't feel anything! I wonder why I used to but don't any more. (sigh) I guess as long as they are getting healed, what's the difference? That is, as long as they are really getting healed and not just saying so for my sake. (Uh oh. There I go again.) You go through a lot of tidal forces out here pulling you one way and then another. I guess that's just the nature of the beast.

But they did get healed. I think the difference with these people is that, unlike Americans, they just simply expect it, so it isn't the great unexpected surprise that it is to us. They carry a simplicity about them that gives them the power to believe.

# 11
# A Funeral in Kumi

Well I heard the bishop preach today, and boy, can he preach! We finished the day at a funeral where hundreds of people had gathered out in an open field. Funerals in East Africa are huge affairs. The main focus of the funeral is always on the preacher, and Bishop Girado did not disappoint. And then, at the end of his message, he divided the crowd in quarters and prayed each section through a Sinners Prayer. And wow, did they pray. At the top of their lungs. It was great.

Yesterday we finished up in Kumi. What a great service we had! (In contrast to the day before.) I could feel the river flowing right from the beginning and it just grew from there. You could feel it coming, and then it hit and picked you up in the flow and carried you away. How do you describe something like that? I listen to some people talk about how good a service was based on what the message was about, but here we're experiencing a flow of the Holy Ghost that lifts you up and carries you higher in the Spirit. Your heart just lifts and flows in the Spirit. It has nothing to do with the words that are said, but it has everything to do with the presence of the Spirit of God. But people from dead churches never seem to understand.

We had a string of testimonies from the healing line yesterday. You should see how excited these people are. Well yeah, duh. They have felt the power of God heal them – some of them from sickness and pain that they have had for a long while – and they are so thankful to God for His mercy. It really grabs your heart to listen to them. These are simple people in deep poverty, afflicted by all sorts of things, but it is that same simplicity that gives rise to a faith without obstructions, restrictions, and complications. They just believe. They don't understand anything else. And so they expect to be healed.

And so they are.

I am done with this part of the trip. A lot of souls got saved during these 3 weeks and a lot of souls got healed. That's pretty exciting, since that's not what I came here to do. I came to ignite churches and start the fires of revival burning. But wherever the Spirit of God is moving, desperate souls will come.

I'm heading for Kampala tomorrow to pick up Cindy and Barry. We will be heading south and west with Pastor Noah for a whole string of services and a whole new set of adventures. I can't wait for them to see these things with their own eyes. Then <u>they</u> can tell you instead of me!

# 12
# A Note from Cindy

This trip to Africa has been very different for Dale. The first three weeks he was in the northern area of Uganda. Barry and I joined him a few days ago in western Uganda. It has been quite an experience for both of us. You will be hearing about all that has happened from a woman's point of view this time!

The first four days were spent in an area where we couldn't get any connection or service for the Internet or our cell phones. That was hard; we weren't expecting that and were just praying that everyone at home would be OK till we could reconnect with them. In the meantime, our basic schedule each day went like this: 8am - 10am the people are praying and singing; preaching is from 10am - 12am; more prayer, more singing; then a lunch break from 1pm – 2pm (that never happened!) and then preaching from 2pm – 4pm; more prayer, more singing and then services are over at 6pm. Even after we go back to the hotel, the congregation stayed longer to keep praying.

This is an intense pace. Dale is under a lot of pressure to "produce". The message is about revival, but not the kind that is scheduled with a lighted sign out front. This revival is the kind that is coming from your heart, catches fire in the church, and spills out the doors to the unsaved souls. In this particular church, many pastors have come from different districts and by the end of the four day session, they have forgotten their differences and have joined together in repentance and prayer, and now are a force to be reckoned with. In the evening, they move to an open-air crusade in town where scores of souls have been getting saved.

The Spirit of the Lord moved in different ways through each service. I honestly didn't know what my "job" was. Dale said just relax, be myself, be there to encourage him, and see what direction the Lord takes me. I needed to hear that.

There is so much to tell that I'll split everything up into small emails. So that being said—I'll explain about staying in a very cool safari lodge, seeing elephants casually walking down the hill outside of the dining area, visiting with Pastor Noah's wife and seeing the street orphans she takes in, and ministering to four women in their home after a terrible tragedy.

# 13
# Into Southern Uganda

It's been a week or so since I've written. A lot has happened, but I was pretty distracted. Cindy and Barry were here and we have had an incredible time. There was no internet connection where we were ministering, so we couldn't make any phone calls back home (which was a real issue for both Barry and Cindy for a while).

Cindy has been to Africa before, but not like this. This was at another level of intensity than what she has seen. And Barry ... Barry is like a little kid, he is so excited. It is so much fun to watch his reaction to everything. Services last all day with no real break in between. The singing and dancing is wild, the times of prayer have been intense, and the preaching has been under the anointing. This is not like anything you will find in the churches back home.

But it's the hunger that really gets him. It has been 40 years since he has seen such hunger for God in people. And to see souls getting saved every day! Wow, is he excited! He is soaking it up like a parched desert in a rainstorm.

We lucked out (if that's what you call it) for our hotel. We are staying in a safari resort with gorgeous accommodations, a high class cuisine restaurant, and personal service. Regular price is $155 per night (and that's here in Uganda where prices are usually 1/3 of what we are used to). Our price? Forty-one bucks a night. Cool. We sit on our veranda outside our beautiful cabin and watch elephants and antelope down below. Yeah, this sure beats the places where I usually stay in with no hot water, intermittent power, and nothing but an iron bed and a plastic chair. Maybe I'm getting old, and maybe I'm getting spoiled, but I don't care. This ain't bad.

Cindy and Barry can tell you the rest. You can call them and I'm sure they would love to tell you the stories. Cindy is home now and Barry will be home on April 6th. I don't know when I'll be able to send this out, but when I can, I'll tell you the rest of what is happening here.

# 14
# Cindy Again

I'm back in Texas, and I'm tired. It's about a 24 hour trip on the planes, in the airports, through the security checkpoints, and finally in the car heading home. Now it's hard to believe I was even in Uganda! But then I think about each service I was in and yes—I was there!

Americans are more reserved in showing their feelings in church; Ugandans have no such inhibitions. But what I witnessed went beyond an emotional response. Each service brought in a new layer of repentance. Almost like peeling the layers of an onion. I was sitting in the front facing the congregation, and I could see understanding, conviction, and fear of God come over their faces. While Dale was preaching, people were leaning forward on their benches with their chins cupped in their hands, and their eyes never moving from his face. They got the message real quick that he didn't care whether they gave him those big "Amen's" and hand clapping. He wanted confirmation that this revival message was being buried deep in their heart. Did they believe that Jesus Christ could overcome witchcraft? Would they read the Bible so they could gain God's power in their lives? Did they accept responsibility for the job of reaching their unsaved neighbors? Were they committed?

I like the fact that Dale gave them a plan in bite-size bits. Read one Proverb a day. Pray for a desire to read. Pray for unsaved souls. Gather your friends together, make some rice and beans, make reading and praying together fun. This gives each person accountability to each other and God. And when there is a bond with each other and God, there will be renewed strength.

The Spirit of God was like a breeze flowing through and around the whole congregation. I could visualize wispy wind tendrils curling around everyone's hearts (even mine!). Barry was so excited he was like a little kid! Noah would be on his feet thanking God. And people were being changed! I witnessed all this and more. So, yes—I was there. I 'm hoping by these letters that I can make you feel like you were there too.

# 15
# On to Western Uganda

I haven't written much about this leg of the journey because I was so taken up with Cindy that I have to admit, you guys didn't enter my mind very much. This was something very special for us. I don't know how to explain it, but it was as if God did something special just for us.

In the meantime, we had 2 and 3 services a day and an open air crusade after. The Lord would give me brand new messages every time. It was really neat how they would develop right out of the air, and how they would be right on target. Throughout the message, these people would be cheering and praising the Lord, arms waving, and faces beaming. You can feel it working. God is planting the seeds of revival here. These people will go back to their churches with a fire in their hearts and spread it to others. I believe that. I really do. You can see in their faces that they have been changed and their entire outlook has been converted. They are fired up to take the focus off themselves and turn it squarely on winning the lost. What better thing could you hope for?

God has accompanied His message with healings also. At least two or three people were crippled and got healed – I mean like throw-away-the-crutches-because-they-can-now-walk type of healed! One guy came up that was paralyzed on one side, arm and leg, and started hollering at me. At first, I couldn't figure out what he wanted. He didn't want anything! He was trying to tell me that God healed him and he was no longer paralyzed! There was a host of others, but we didn't call for testimonies so I'm not sure what some of them were, but the thing that really gets me is that they weren't healed in a healing line with someone anointing them with oil and praying over them. They were healed during the services just by the presence of the Holy Spirit. Yeah. It was that good!

This seems to be increasing every trip I take. It's as if there is a crescendo building with God's people and He is rising up within them like a burgeoning ground swell of desperation, faith, and hope for revival. The services are becoming more powerful and the miracles are becoming greater and more plentiful. Maybe it's just my imagination, but I think God is about ready to break out of the box.

I'd like to tell you all about what Africa is like and give you a tour guide of what it is like here, but honestly, all I pay attention to is the services … and Cindy. I guess I've been coming for so long that I don't even notice things any more. Or maybe it's just that the excitement about an impending revival here outshines everything else.

Wish you were here to see it for yourself. (and I mean that for everyone)

# 16
# In Kihihi

Wow. Services today were beyond belief! It was like something you read about in a book about revivals. Something broke through today and these people will never be the same.

This has been Day 4 in a village called Kihihi, way out on the western edge of Uganda. Zaire is only a few miles down the road. There are gorillas somewhere around here that tourists come to see, but other than that, while it is not exactly remote, this place is pretty rural. Nobody ever comes here to hold Gospel meetings, never mind a white guy from America. But then, these are the kinds of places that the Lord has been sending me to for six years now, so what else is new?

People have been coming from everywhere, filling the place up. The church is a rude affair of sticks cobbled together to form the walls and roof and covered with a huge plastic tarp that has "US Aid" printed all over it. When it rains, it leaks all over. But that doesn't stop anyone – they just keep coming.

For three days the intensity has been increasing. Services start at 10am and last straight through until 2pm. That includes lots of singing and praying out loud and not one, but two messages from me. Then we come back after lunch at 4pm for the third service, and then immediately go into the open air crusade outside until late at night. I go back to the hotel after the third service to recharge my battery, but Barry goes out to preach at the crusade. Two hundred souls have been saved here in the last few days – that's 200, as in two hundred!

The excitement in the air can be felt in the reverberations that come from the praying. No, praying is not quite a strong enough word. It's more like intense war, the thick of combat, the smoke of battle and the victory that only strong faith can lay claim to. Our revival prayer meetings back in the States are anemic in comparison. And this is just during the regular service! When I call for repentance and rededication at the end of the message it is like unleashing a storm! You just cannot imagine what it is like unless you are here to experience it.

Tonight was the last service for me. Before leaving, I wanted to at least have a time of prayer for healing sicknesses, both physical and spiritual. Pastor Noah started off by asking for testimonies, and a whole bunch of them came up to tell the things that had happened to them - some spiritual, some about the things they had learned, and some about how they got healed during the services. And THEN we started the healing line.

Let me just say that the more I prayed over them, the longer the line got. (It's always that way). We started with the usual aches, pains, and headaches. All those pains left. Then came a whole array of more serious things, like bleedings and paralyzed limbs. Gone. And then came a man who was deaf. (Oh Lord, I need some help here. This would be a good time for you to show up. I don't know why I think it is easier to heal headaches than deafness, but Lord, everybody is watching so please help me out here.)

I didn't really know what to do, but I had heard somewhere about a guy sticking his fingers in a deaf person's ears and praying over him. Sounded like a good idea to me, so that's what I did. I even popped my fingers out of his ear for a dramatic effect. (Was that supposed to help?) Nada, nope, nothing. Still can't hear. Not to be denied, I prayed again (this time without the finger popping), and I prayed hard.

Pastor Noah started walking backwards from him, "Can you hear me now?" "Yes".

A little further back, "Can you hear me now?" "Yes"

And so on, all the way to the back of the church. Way back there, I could barely hear Noah, but this deaf man heard him perfectly!

Am I jazzed? Ya think? Somewhere about 20 to 30 people got healed – almost everyone that came up. Yes, there was one boy with a large tumor that, when I prayed over him, did not disappear. Maybe it will later, I don't know, but it didn't vanish on the spot like I expected. That's a real bummer, but I don't know what else to do. Maybe this gift of healing is a thing that grows as your faith expands.

I hope so, because the look of desperate relief on the faces of the people who did get healed is priceless.

Something huge happened in Kihihi. Huge. You could feel it in the air like something broke through some long established spiritual walls. Old theological ideas were smashed, personal wants were traded for a burden for lost souls, and a long ago buried faith that had been almost smothered by a mediocre church burst out of the grave and rose again in people's hearts. They will never be the same ... ever.

Neither will I.

# 17
# Holding Back the Rain

I just got off the phone with Dale. They have finished the services at the Kihihi church. He said to tell everyone that they are "on the move." There have been over 200 souls saved in 3 days. Dale preaches at the first two services and Barry preaches at the open air service in the evening. There have been healings like you wouldn't believe. Someone who was deaf was healed! They asked him to go about 10 feet away, can he hear them? YES. Ten more feet away, can he hear them? YES. Ten more feet (all the way to the back of the building), can he hear them? YES!

So needless to say—the Spirit is so thick you can cut it with a knife! The people who get these emails, who support this ministry with money, and who support us with prayers—you are getting stars added to your crowns.

There has been so much mental turmoil and insane problems

both in our office and out on the front line in Africa. We realize that in the spiritual world, there are strongholds being destroyed, but when crazy stuff happens, how many times can we blame the devil? Is the office equipment breaking down like this normal? When our phones don't work or they get stolen, is that normal? Is it really Satan pulling out his entire arsenal to discourage us? YES.

If we are reassured that people are contending before the Lord for this ministry, then we feel better. It's easy to believe when you are watching it happen right before your eyes. It's harder to believe back here in America. I'm hoping these letters make it a little easier to believe.

We were told that people were praying to hold back the rain at the Bunyarugu church until after the 4 day "conference" was over. We wouldn't have been able to drive on the crazy roads if they were muddy. Guess when the rain started? YES—you guessed it—just minutes after the last morning service as we were driving away.

Another praying group at the church in Nyakashebeya had been praying that Dale and his "team" would be able to come to their church also. And there we were! After services, they came to the altar for special prayer. They thought they were blessed; we knew we were blessed. Does prayer work? YES!

I still need to tell about spending the afternoon with Noah's wife and about dedicating someone's baby to the Lord. So expect more letters!

# 19
# The Hem of His Garment

The intensity and violent outpourings of the Holy Spirit is what I am finding extraordinary on this trip. I've had services before that were so anointed that you felt like you were floating, where people could actually <u>see</u> the glow of the Shekinah Glory. I've had healing lines where EVERBODY got healed, and services where the church we were at doubled and tripled in numbers within a week or so. But there is something deeper about this trip that I have not sensed before. Maybe that's why I have gone through so much fire.

Yesterday and today really put a point on things. We were way out in the mountain villages. At first, I was a little dismayed yesterday as we struggled through an hour of mountain dirt roads to end up at some little church on top of a mountain. Here we had come all this way, spent all this money, time, and energy (that I was just about out of by now), for this little tiny church? Why didn't someone tell us that it was going to be such a small crowd way out in the middle of nowhere! (Can you tell I'm getting worn out and cranky?)

Stupid me. I should have had a clue when I saw all the tarps strung out over the field. But at least I sucked it up, knowing that I have been in this situation before and have seen God pour out incredible anointings on these little tiny settings ... just like with

Cornelius in Acts 10. It has happened to me more times than I can remember.

Sure enough, here they came. From all over, for miles around, walking for hours to get there. It wasn't the number of people that got me - it was the intensity of their desperate hunger for God that really grabbed me. Preaching to this crowd was like dropping a match on a tank of gasoline. Where does that kind of intensity come from? How do you describe the workings of the Spirit that takes place in the realm of the soul? I honestly don't know. I don't think I will ever know. I just stand there amazed.

And then came the healings. At the end of the second service on the first day, Pastor Noah called for everyone to place their hand on wherever the pain was as I got up to pray for the healing. There were a lot of healings. Several people came up to tell us of the debilitating things that they got instantly healed of, but one guy came forward who had a broken arm. You could see the bump where the break was. He couldn't pick anything up, couldn't twist it or put it behind his back, or even touch anything. It was really broken ... until we prayed. When he put his hand on where the pain was, God also put

His hand on it and healed it completely in an instant. He could hardly believe his own eyes! God really does do the supernatural.

Today, however, was even more special. As far as I'm concerned, healing the blind is right up there with raising the dead. It's always scary for me to pray over someone who is blind. I'm sorry, but I have a real struggle with the challenge to my faith when that happens. And yet, earlier this year I had prayed over an old lady who was blind when I prayed over her. Still ...

So I was in my "Oh God, help me, I'm scared" mode when they brought up a man who had lost his sight two years ago. So I prayed. And prayed, and prayed, and prayed. Can't feel anything. And I can't ask him anything because he doesn't speak English. So I prayed some more. Then Noah prayed over him. Then we both prayed. Noah asked him if he could see, and he said he could begin to make out fuzzy shapes. Whoa! That's just like in Mark 8 when Jesus prayed over the guy and he could barely make out shapes. Now I'm encouraged. This just might really happen!

We prayed some more, and now he could see better – not perfect, but better. Noah held out his hand, and the guy saw it and shook it. Noah told him to follow him as he backed up and then turned, and the guy followed him into the turn. He could see! Yeah, you heard me. He could see!

Why am I so surprised? It is one thing to talk about this happening to someone else; it's entirely another thing to be faced with this kind of a supreme challenge to your faith. I have made it through many times to see God do things that were supernatural, but living in a carnal world casts a shade upon you that keeps supernatural faith at arm's length. You have to reach hard for it every time. I don't know if it was me, Noah, or the blind man, but somebody reached out and touched the hem of His garment.

I wish you could see some of the things we are experiencing here almost every day. This is really happening. God is moving in incredible ways. I have said it over and over and will say it again - the last great revival prophesied in the Book of Joel and Isaiah will begin in Africa because they are so desperately hungry for God, and He will use them to send the fire around the world. I believe I am seeing the very beginnings of that Great African Revival.

# 20
# Back in Mbarara

We are back in Mbarara, Pastor Noah's hometown. I am running on fumes, worn out deep inside. I gave the Sunday message and then stood up again in the evening to give a sort of intro message because many people are still on their way here. I could barely stand. And besides that, I had no idea what to say. I am drained, my bucket is empty, and I have nothing more to give. I just wanted to get it over with, say something cursory, and get out of there.

It is times like this that you realize your mortality and the utter weakness of your flesh. "Oh God, please remember that this is not about me, but about your sheep. Feed your sheep – that's what you told Peter and I'm throwing it back on You because I don't have anything more to give."

Sure enough, it was one of the best messages I've given. Happens every time. When you are weakest, He becomes strong.

In the evening, Noah's brother David and his wife came to the hotel to talk to us. I know them from last year, but Barry had not heard their testimony. She was from Rwanda and her entire family was massacred. Something I said during the service broke the hatred and unforgiveness that had a hold inside her heart. Not sure what I said, but she told us that God had sent me just for her. It changed her life. (Sigh) That just feels good. I don't know how else to say it.

David was just 10 when Idi Amin's police hauled off his mother and father to prison for preaching the Gospel and kidnapped his older brother. He turned into a "street kid" for the next several years, living on the street, eating garbage, and strung out on drugs. He hated God and hated Christians. But someone came and showed him love and compassion – no preaching or anything heavy, just making friends, bringing bananas to eat and a ball to play soccer with. He finally made it back to the Lord and now runs an orphanage out of his house, taking in lost kids off the streets. What a testimony! Makes me feel humbled just to be with them.

And get this – they think the same of me because I am bringing a message of revival that is revolutionizing the churches here. My friend Barry was a little put off by that, but I told him that you just have to go with it. It's not about us – it's a deep embedded hope and need in their hearts that God will visit them with mercy and send a real, Holy Ghost revival. I'm just the guy who is the front man with the message. If they only realized how little I really am.

There were three services today. I have no idea where the messages are coming from, but they are not coming from me. I am out of gas. I am so tired that I feel like I am just walking forward but

not knowing where I am going. But as I am getting ready to get up and get behind the pulpit, I can feel this thing come down on me. Not sure what it was, but I broke out in tears. It felt like my heart swelled up in my throat. It's okay – God is in charge. Just get up there and open your mouth and He will fill it. I feel like I am standing on the edge of a high cliff and all I have to do is stretch my wings and dive and let the wind of God lift my wings and fly.

Whenever you are preaching under the anointing, it is like a river that is rushing through you. You feel nothing else – no back pain, no fatigue, no sickness, no stomach ache. Many times I can gauge how good the message will be by how bad I feel before I get up there. But once you get up, it is like you step into a zone, and you feel nothing. Until it's over. And then you are completely drained.

And that is where I am right now. Good night. I am going to bed.

# 21
# Delivering the Message

There is a huge difference between the north of Uganda and the south. The north is dry and brown; the south is green and lush. Towns in the north are small, mostly one-street towns with dirt roads running into the Bush. They all have a lazy slouch to them, like a sleepy Mexican town out in the desert. Mostly, they're just waiting for the rain.

But the feel of the air, especially in the morning, is something special. It is clear and crisp, the sunlight is direct, and yet there is that distinct tropical feel to the air. But by noon, it has burned off and you want to be standing in the shade. You can get a sunburn fast out here.

I guess the people are pretty much the same. It's hard for me to tell. I've met folks from so many different tribes with names I can't pronounce that I can't tell the difference. But they are all the nicest folks you could ever meet. They are genuinely thrilled to meet us. True, part of it is being a white man from America (they worship the idea of America over here), but really, most of it is that they are just a bunch of decent, simple people. There is little sign of aggressiveness in them, which works both ways. While their peaceable nature means they shy away from arguments, it also shows up in a lack of initiative. It's part of the cultural difference between Africa and the West, and I'm not so sure we got the better side of it.

The hardest part of the mission is always the struggle with having to deliver an anointed message every day, sometimes 2 and 3 times a day. Anybody can deliver a message – that's easy if you don't care that much – but to feel the weight of responsibility to deliver a message that is anointed from the Throne of God that comes directly from Him is a whole 'nother story. You have to maintain a level of intensity every day that is high in the Spirit and with a sharp cutting edge. There is no room for failure. Mistakes, as our pastor once said, in this business are fatal. You HAVE to deliver. You HAVE to be in the Spirit. You HAVE to pierce their hearts. It is a matter of Eternity.

When you have to do this every day, it begins to wear on you. While the basic messages of revival that I've been bringing have been pretty much the same, nevertheless, each time I stand up behind the pulpit, it is a brand new experience, and somehow, a brand new message. It's not the words that are important – it's the power with which you speak them. What's that Scripture? "The kingdom of God is not in word, but in power." Yeah, that's the difference.

After 4 or 5 weeks and about a hundred or so messages, you feel like there is nothing left in the bucket to pour out, but the Lord always shows up. It just blows my mind sometimes. I figure that somebody must be praying pretty heavily because it sure isn't coming from me. I'm spent. I just have to suck it up and keep going. The harder it gets and the less strength I have to put into it, the more God takes over until I reach the point where I finally let go, stand back, and watch God shine.

That's a small price to pay to get to be up front and close with the miraculous and watch lives transform.

# 22
# Intensity in Mbarara

It's Sunday night in Mbarara. I am drained, but Noah makes the statement that it doesn't matter because God will not forsake His people and He will give me a supernatural message. I'm sure glad Noah is so reassured because I have no idea what I will say and I'm too tired to care. I was just going to do some sort of a cheap intro for what I will talk about during the next few days and then run off to the hotel.

Um, not quite. I ended up pouring my heart out like I have not done in a long time. You just wonder where this stuff comes from sometimes.

The place is packed, but I can feel something binding up the service. First it was some crazy woman that I pleaded the Blood of Jesus against and commanded the demons to leave. She doesn't speak English, but I guess the demons do because she immediately got up and shot out the back door. But there is something else here, like a spirit of slumber. Pastor Kibedi realizes that half the place speaks one language and the other half another language. No wonder half the place was bored! The solution? Preach with a second translator! So now I have to speak a phrase and then wait while first one and then the other spit out their translations. If that sounds rough, it is, but it frees everything up because now we have everyone's attention. Actually, once we got in a rhythm, it wasn't too bad.

By the third day, we have reached an intensity that you never see in American churches. When they start to pray, it is so loud that the noise level over amps your ears. And they keep going and going. They are on their feet, waving their hands, some of them shaking or jumping up and down… for a long time. It is so foreign to Western Christianity that you can start to wonder if it is really real, but it is more than real. There are no baffles or insulating layers to the African soul to dampen the intensity of this storm that is pouring out

of their hearts. It's just that they are desperate.

This is not a prayer of praise or thanksgiving but of a deep, heart-wrenching cry of repentance, desperate to take hold of the horns of the altar and cry out to God from the depths of their hearts. It is a cry that pierces your soul and tears into the very foundations of Heaven to shake the Throne of God. You have never heard such a soul-piercing cry. It lasted a solid hour at the top of their lungs, weeping, jumping, marching, contending, and crying out to their Father in Heaven.

How can God possibly refuse these people a revival?

# 23
# Cindy and Diana

Noah is Dale's host and has done a tremendous job of organizing the church conferences, hotels, and car rental. But the schedule was so packed that I didn't know when I was going to have time to visit with his wife, Diana. But he did have a day off figured in, so I spent the afternoon with Diana at their house. They have been married about three years; she is 22 and he is 30. So think about that—Christy is 18; can I picture her being married right now to someone 8 years older than her? Not hardly.

Noah was there for a short while, and they both kept saying they couldn't believe that Dale's wife was actually sitting in their home! When Noah left to travel with Barry to the next church, then we talked about all kinds of girl stuff! We were both curious about each other's countries; common day-to-day life; and that sort of thing.

Diana and I told each other the stories of how our husbands courted us! That was funny. The Lord put a love in my heart for Dale the first time I saw him. It took about a year for him to realize that we were meant for each other. We got married six days after he asked me to marry him. Maybe I was afraid that he would change his mind! Noah saw Diana and asked her father if he could talk to her. When she found out he was a pastor she thought, oh my gosh, pastors are poor. They went out on a date (he bought her a soda), and they were married a couple of months later!

An amazing thing about Diana is that she had two orphans that she had "adopted" when she and Noah met. She had found a little

girl sleeping and eating in a trash can. Diana was 13; the little girl was about four. She didn't have a name, didn't know her parents, and didn't have any clothes. Diana took her home as her daughter. She found two little boys a few years later in pretty much the same situation. They had dug holes in the red dirt on the side of the road and that's where they slept. She and Noah now have five children, plus their baby girl who is a little over a year old. I met Trefonn (who is 13 now) and the two boys. The other two children were at day school. Her dream is to someday have a big house with lots of rooms and a yard where children can run around and play. One of Noah's brothers and his wife, David and Esther, have 11 orphan children. All of these children have a new life because of the love of

Diana and Esther.

We spent about 5 hours together. I bought some necklaces and earrings that she had made. We had lunch. We teased each other and got serious with each. She took me to a friend's house so I could encourage and bless two women whose husbands had recently died. That is a letter all by itself.

Since both our husbands are intense and full of fire and zeal with a burden of God on their hearts, we definitely had something in common. Being with Dale on this trip has been an eye-opener for me. The way the Spirit flows through services and the way the messages filled the hearts of the people in the congregation touched my heart. Wishing our husbands were home more often doesn't seem so important when we can see the life changing work they are immersed in. It is not always possible to be with them as they travel around, but when we are able to, it is GOOD!

# 24
# Royalty in God

We are way off the main road, holding our revival services in a church right on top of a mountain overlooking the Queen Elizabeth National Park. The road up here to this church is narrow, winding, and full of ruts and holes. Lord help us if it rains!

You got to wonder where the people are going to come from (actually, I wonder this almost every time), but so many people have come ( between 200 to 300) that they have to stretch a huge canvas supported by poles outside the church to accommodate everyone. This is a long hard walk up a steep mountain for these people to get here, but I don't think any of them care. They just want to hear the Word of God. When you look out over the crowd, the Scripture from the Beatitudes really hits you, "Blessed are the poor in spirit for theirs is the Kingdom of Heaven". These people don't have all the scintillating distractions we have in America, so their souls are open to the Kingdom of Heaven. What a very different thing we have here!

The first couple of services in these meetings are always hard. I have to snap their illusions and bring them to a realization that "church as usual" is not good enough. No matter how good they think their church is, if souls are not coming to the altar in any real numbers, they just simply do not have a revival – they just have church. It is not hard to convince them. They already know this. That's why they are here. The hard question is not whether they are satisfied, but whether they are willing to pay the high price to bring revival. My core Scripture is always Genesis 30:1, "Give me souls, lest I die!" You have to want it so bad that you are willing to die, to give your life to see souls get saved. Anything less and you will not be willing to do what it takes to have a real revival.

They don't care. They were willing to walk up the side of a mountain to get here and they are willing to do whatever it takes to have a revival. It's like they are right in the palm of my hand, sitting on the edge of their seats, taking in everything I tell them. Just tell them more ... and please don't stop talking. Lord, where have You been hiding these people?

Some wrinkled old woman has pushed her way through the crowd to where I am sitting and kneels down in front of me. She is jabbering away like crazy and pushes a 1,000 shilling note in my hand. That's about 40 cents, but you can bet it's a lot of money to her. She keeps pointing at her arms and her veins – something about her blood or something – and then just up and hugs me in a bear hug. Apparently, this old woman had been very, very sick for a long time and the Lord had told her that if she would just come to the service, He would heal her. She came in while I was praying and, sure enough, got healed. This was one excited old woman!

This church is pastored by Noah's sister, Ruth, and her husband. Ruth can sing. I mean like, really sing. During the song, "Jesus, Be Thou Glorified", she touched places in my heart that have not been touched in forty years. I was floating way out there somewhere in the Spirit … and didn't want to come back down.

This whole family is royalty. That's the impression the Lord gave me about them today. The father and mother were having revivals in Uganda when Idi Amin threw them both in jail, leaving 9 little kids to fend for themselves in the bush. An oppressive culture of fear had swept over the land and few would do anything to help them. The father, Elijah, thought he'd never see his children or his wife again. The oldest, just a young teen-ager, was taken and thrown in jail, and the second oldest thought he would be next, so at 10 yrs. old, he left for the streets of the city where he became a street kid for years. The younger kids were scattered because the government took their home. They were finally delivered, but what a price to pay.

They never forsook their faith in the face of imprisonment, torture, and the destruction of their family. God spoke to the father and told him not to despair, that all his children would be preaching the Gospel, and he would see revival come to Uganda with his own two eyes. It has happened just like God told him – all his children are in ministry, and here I come along with this hard-hitting message of revival accompanied with this special anointing that comes down on every service we've had like he hasn't felt since the 70's. You can just imagine how excited he and his wife are.

These people have paid a price that I can't even hold a candle to. I look at them and I see a family that is royalty in God's family. His children are princes and princesses. My guess is that there's a lot of this here in Uganda. I reckon we will be surprised to see who is really who when we get on the other side.

# 25
# Healings and One-Liners

By now everyone should be getting something from Dale about the districts that he has traveled to after I came home. I'm still writing about the two places that I was at.

I'm glad that I got to witness all that Dale has been telling me about for the last few years. I told him I know how he preaches because every time he reads and the Lord shows him something in the Bible, he preaches to me. He is expected to preach 2-3 services a day for several days in a row with no break, and there is no time for a prepared message with notes. I watched him read and pray and sometimes worry; but when he stood up in front of everybody it felt like a mantel settled on his shoulders. He was ready to feed to the congregation what God had just fed him. It's amazing to watch this right on the spot. And there were times when I could see all over his face, that whatever he thought he was going to say had just been replaced by what God wanted him to say. And he'll say "WOW" and tell them—the Lord just gave me that to give to you. Is that cool or what!

The healing part is another story. We don't want to fail God; we want everyone to believe; we know that we are just flesh. I was asked to pray for a woman who couldn't bear children. God please help me and her. Please God—touch these people for whatever they need. I saw joy on people's faces even if I couldn't understand what their problem was or understand what they were saying. A man whose arm was paralyzed kept raising it and shouting at us. Finally Noah explained what happened to him. A teenage boy said that bad demons would talk to him at night; but when he asked Jesus Christ to wash his soul in His blood, then the demons went away and he had peace. An older lady had so much trouble walking that she would move on her hands and knees because it hurt too much to stand up straight. She was standing up straight, raising her hands, and telling us how God healed her. She even got down on her knees to show us how she had been walking when she came into the church. Needless to say—she was EXCITED! There were lots more in the two churches I went to and even more after I left. Healings don't save souls and miracles don't save souls. But souls were getting saved and God was healing people!

I call some of what Dale preaches one-liners. "It's not about you, it's about others." "Quit thinking about your problems, and

pray for the souls who are heading for hell." "You say you want a revival? There's a price to pay. Do you want to pay it?" "Is it hard for you to read? Then ask God for a desire and a burden to read and He'll give it to you." "I'm counting on you for this revival, because America needs to be revived."

I do not know how God will make a revival jump across the Atlantic Ocean to the States from a village church in Uganda but after witnessing the Spirit moving on these people, I just have to believe that it will.

# 26
# Miracles and Anointing

I'd like to say something about the miracles. There have been a lot of incredible miracles, especially on this trip. They have ranged from the blind and deaf to issues of blood and paralysis. There have also been a few that are a little too weird to relate here. But the focus of all my campaigns out here is not about miracles – it's about revival.

Miracles are wonderful and are like God's seal of approval on your ministry, but miracles do not convert the soul, change your heart, or save you. Only the Word of God can do that.

One time in Nigeria, the Lord told me, "No miracles. If you do the miracles, they will not hear the message." Just like that. Right out of the clear blue sky. In spite of that, God still did two miracles, but I got the message. I believe that this is the real problem with these huge international healing ministries. They got focused on the wrong thing, became enamored with the blessings, and forgot the purpose for which they were called – to preach the Gospel and win souls – and they have ended up making a circus of a very holy gift from God.

Instead of leading the Body of Christ to the altar so that God can move in our lives and in our churches, they instead are leading us in another direction, away from the altar of repentance and toward a focus on self – what blessings God will give us, what is in it for ourselves, what problems that we want God to fix ... gimme, gimme, gimme. I call it the Gospel of Me. But no revival comes without deep, broken-hearted repentance at the altar. So instead of bringing health to the Church, they are leading them into folly like a Pied Piper playing an alluring but dangerous melody.

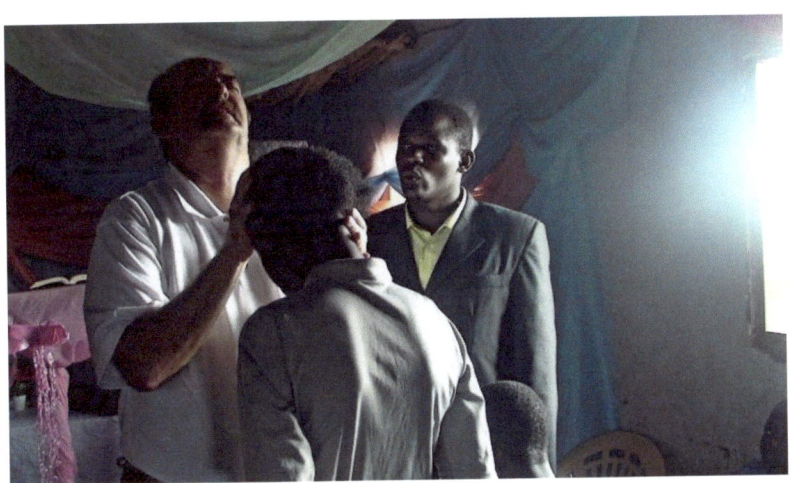

Nevertheless, it is certainly gratifying to see real, honest-to-goodness miracles happen right in front of your eyes. I may be excited about it, but you should see the look on the face of someone who has really been healed of some disease, or pain, or crippling infirmity when it is gone, completely gone, eliminated, whoosh!

Then there are the people who, when you touch them, you can feel the anointing flow. I can't explain it, but you know that something special just happened to that person. Some of them shake, some swoon, some sway back and forth, and some just melt, but all of them are irrevocably affected. You know God has done something to them that goes deeper than the flesh and into the issues of the heart. They have, on some deeper spiritual level, been changed. On this trip I have seen the blind see, the deaf hear, the crippled walk, and a myriad of other diseases and infirmities healed, but I think these spiritual anointings, while very mysterious, are the greater miracles.

These things don't happen naturally, not even here in Africa, but when the oil starts flowing in the service, you can feel the Anointing in the air ... and that is even more exciting.

Perhaps there is something here that is related to the finger of God preparing hearts to receive this coming revival. Who knows? Certainly not me. I just show up and watch as God deals supernaturally with His people. But I sure am glad to be here to see it.

# 27
# Going Home

Well, it is finally over and I am over the middle of the Atlantic, on my way home. These seven weeks have not felt terribly long – maybe because Cindy had come over during the middle of it, but I really think that it is because so much was happening that I just did not have time to get homesick.

It seems that the intensity of the workings of the Spirit is increasing with each new trip that I take. There have been a lot of incredible services over the past six years, and I have been in several meetings where the Holy Ghost literally fell out of the sky on us, but it just seemed like this particular trip has maintained a high level of intensity throughout every service in every place we went. Maybe God is picking up the pace because the time is getting short. Or maybe I'm just getting better at this. Or maybe I have just not been paying attention. Whatever the reason, I get the overwhelming sense that we are stepping into a new level.

The message hasn't changed that much. It is still the basic "Four Steps to Revival", although it has certainly matured since I first wrote the booklet, and there have been many more new insights from new passages in the Bible. Still, something has changed and I honestly think it has more to do with how little time is left than anything else.

I preached close to 100 messages to well over a thousand people, somewhere around 300 souls got saved, and at least 100 or so people got healed of a wide variety of problems. We gave out over 200 Bibles in their indigenous languages and over a thousand of the "Four Steps to Revival" booklets. All of that sounds great, but the real question is will all this have a long lasting impact? What did we accomplish and how long will it last?

I believe we did something that touched Eternity; something that went deeper into God's Plan than we can see right now. It's as if we are in the river and another stream entered into the flow and the river has now picked up steam. The press of the end times is upon us.

Bishop Girado, my host for the first three weeks in northern Uganda, called me to tell me that all the churches I preached in are still on fire, many are having services everyday now, and are winning souls. Pastor Noah, my host in southern Uganda, is also getting calls from the churches there that are full to capacity and are actively pursuing lost souls. Ruth, the pastor at the church on the mountaintop, called me to tell me that "It is working. The fire is burning. Revival has begun in Uganda."

That's what makes it all worthwhile. That's what keeps me going back. Yes, it can be difficult at times, exhausting, frustrating, and sometimes lonely, but it's working, the fire is burning, and revival has begun. What else could you ask for?

# About the Author

Dalen Garris has been in ministry since 1970 during the Jesus Movement in California. He started a radio broadcast in 1997 that was heard on stations around the world for almost 12 years. A newspaper column followed, for which he has written over 700 articles, which were published in newspapers and Christian magazines in several countries. He has also written several books and booklets.

Since 2004, he has been lighting the fires of revival in churches spread across sub-Saharan Africa. During the course of 14 years, he has preached in over 700 churches, seen hundreds of churches have been set on fire, hundreds of people have been supernaturally healed, and tens of thousands have been saved. And the fires are still burning.

Because of his work across Africa, Dalen Garris was awarded an honorary Doctorate in 2017 by the Northwestern Christian University of Florida.

Dr. Garris currently lives with Cindy, his wife of 40 years, in Waxahachie and is still heavily involved with orphanages and churches across Africa. His pressing hope is in seeing this upcoming generation be the Gideon Generation that will usher in this last, great revival that he has preached about for so many years.

## Contact Information

# Dalen Garris

## *Revivalfire Ministries*

PO Box 822, Waxahachie, TX 75168

http://RevivalFire.org

dale@revivalfire.org

## **Other Books by Dalen Garris**

Fire in the Hole
The Kenya Diaries
Do You Have Eternal Security
Two Covenants

## **Other Booklets from Ministry Trips**

10 Days in Nairobi
Volcano in Cape Verde
A Light in the Bush
A Trumpet in Nigeria
Into the Heart of Darkness
Uganda, 2011
Tanzania, 2011
Nigeria, 2012
Planting a Seed in Liberia
A Whisper in the Wind
Revival Services in Rwanda & Burundi